THE ISSUE

THE ISSUE

Volume IX
2014 to 2016

Arthur R. Marinello

PREFACE

It is a privilege to live this life. To be living in such a way as to experience the precious, its preciousness revealed in the heartache of loss. To have experienced the humanity therein. To know saints walking quietly among us. To have known the joyful ones. And to look sadly on the lives lived tragically, their value, their preciousness evident in their waste. Yes, a privilege to know all this richness.

A.R.M.

TABLE OF CONTENTS

THE STRUGGLE

4:25 pm, Friday
December 19, 2014

I wonder
I wonder
Does the soul struggle
For acknowledgement

The body has the
Primary place
In the consciousness
Ever struggling
Ever complaining

And the soul struggles
Struggles

An uneven battle

The struggle continues
To gain recognition
To have its rightful place

To sense
To feel
To guide

LIFE HAS

11:10 am, Sunday
December 21, 2014

Life has its requirements
Does that surprise you?

Well
It does

What are those requirements?
How do I know?

Anyway
Let's see

Honesty, obviously
And sanctity
And courage
Love and compassion
And relatedness

We are all related, after all

There's humility
It's not much of a life
Without humility

And a search for beauty
And joy
Etc.

OVERALL PATTERN APPRAISAL

7:34 am, Thursday
Christmas Day, Dec. 25, 2014

The term "delayed gratification"
Has only in recent years
Come to my attention

But, last night,
Christmas Eve,
It came to the fore

An incident
Or series of incidents
Or issue
Or series of issues
Presented themselves

And so it was that
A new awareness
For me
Came to be

And with it
A new term
For me
And that is "Overall Pattern Appraisal"

And that is
If you could see or feel
The totality of an issue
It would give you pause

New Orleans

I WASN'T LOOKING

9:25 am, Saturday
January 3, 2015

I was just now
Sitting in my library
Listening to some music
By Vaughn-Williams

Thinking that I might
Do some thinking
But no
Nothing
And then I realized
That most of the
Inspirations
That come my way

Do not occur
As you might think

No--------
They come
You might say
When I'm not looking

When,
So far as I can tell
I had little to do
With them

TREES

5:30 pm, Friday
January 30, 2015

One of the most
Beautiful sights for me
Is when
Sitting in my library
And looking out the windows
Facing West
And seeing the trees

Looking beyond
The fruit trees
In my back yard

And seeing the high trees
The large trees
So tall

There is something about them
That gives me pleasure
That exudes calmness
Permanence
Beauty

There is something
About trees

MAD AT ME

7:08 pm, Monday
February 2, 2015

This morning I had
A grapefruit
A half of one
And it was delicious
And juicy
Rather special

A year or more ago
The tree this fruit
Came from
Had not produced any fruit
For something like four years
And I decided to
Get rid of it

So I bought another
Grapefruit tree
And planted it

As I was about
To throw the older one out
I suddenly changed my mind
And decided to plant it
Somewhere else

The result was that
It outperformed the new tree
With two or three times
As much fruit

This morning I called Dean
My nurseryman
To tell him about a fig tree
I bought a year or so ago
That was doing poorly

And when I divulged to him
That I'd planted it
In a wine barrel
And that in heavy rains
The barrel had become flooded
For a few or more hours
Which apparently was not good
For the fig tree
He said

That the fig tree
Was mad at me

NO RECOURSE

2:13 pm, Thursday
February 26, 2015

And so, here it is
I was told this story
I wasn't being nosey
Well no, that's not true
I can be nosey
I was nosey
I typically am

And now I'm stuck
With this tale
Of an incident
That took place
Some decades ago

The kind of incident
I am told
That could well be
Taking place
This day

Though I may be
Mistaken

The teller of this tale
Related to the victim

There was, is,
A shepherd
And like you'd expect
He had these sheep

Very likely he'd been
Warned
And held his ground

At some point
His sheep and his
Horse
Were stolen

Being of a gentle nature
Vulnerable
And having little or no
Recourse
To the law

He was stuck
Any effort he might make
Would entail
Peril
To his family
As well as himself

One day he recognized
His saddle
In town

Still no recourse
He could say
Or do
Nothing

This was Sicily
Some decades ago

And any attempt
To right the wrong
Would be,
Is,
Perilous

Sicily

IT'S COMPLEX

8:23 pm, Monday
March 3, 2015

I tell you
Living with a woman
Is a complex thing

There is a great difference

A man will address
A situation
Directly

Only to be told
It's not the thing to do

Women
Woman
Will say something
That is really not true

Although, I suppose
There is a kind of truth
To it

And to make this matter
Quite astonishing
Other women know
The real truth behind
The cover words

And so
Men are left
In the dark

Perpetually so

I tell you
Living with a woman
Is different
It's complex

And for some reason
For some reason
I intuitively know
That life with
A man
Would be
Is
Intolerable

And, what can I say,
Only a woman
Could manage it

MONEY

11:34 am, Tuesday
March 10, 2015

Money
Money
Money

What can I say about
Money

I think we all know
What money is
But there's more to it

Money enables us to
Obtain the necessities
That might be difficult
To obtain without it

It supplies us with
Some sense of security
A sense of security
That says we can continue
To obtain those necessities

And not having that
Money
Could be a problem

And so
We seek to
Have that security
Which money provides

But there are at least
Two kinds of money

The money to do
The aforementioned
Necessities

And the money that
Unknowingly
Unconsciously
Becomes an end
In itself
And is not used
As an aid to living
And may even
Not be used
Becoming dead money

While the opportunity
To use it as
Live money
Is lost

THE SQUIRRELS

6:16 pm, Thursday
March 12, 2015

Just now
I was sitting on my patio
In sunny southern California

And I noticed a young squirrel
Traversing a high wire

It might well be
The offspring
Of a pair of squirrels
That had been
A blight on my
Crop of fruit
From some of my dozen
Fruit trees

And five or six months ago
I began to hope
That some hawk
Would come by and rid me
Of the older squirrels
And, somehow, they disappeared

But, then again,
Here comes junior
To take up where his parents
Have left off

Pope John Paul II

THE SOCIAL SKILLS

4:12 pm, Friday
March 12, 2015

This morning I dreamt
Of Dolores Sherlock
It may have been
Four or five o'clock
And we
My wife and I
Were visiting her
At what seemed to be
A community on the way
To San Diego

Dolores died many years ago
Ten, fifteen years or more
And the dream was
A pleasant one

When I awoke
At about five thirty
I had, you might say,
A special glimpse
Of Anton Bruckner
An Austrian composer
Of symphonies
Symphonies I'm fond of

He lived in the
Eighteen hundreds

Brilliant though he was
He was considered by some
To be an idiot

He sought to get
Married
A number of times
And failed

I suppose, seriously,
That he lacked
The barest of social skills
To entice a woman
To marry him----
And he was sad

I had never before
Given it much thought
Beyond my awareness
Of these facts

But this morning
I could see that
He was something
Like the autistic person
Whom we now know
Can be brilliant
While bereft of the
Social skills
The relational skills

CHE COS'HAI FATTU

5:02 pm, Sunday
March 15, 2015

He was crumbling
Disintegrating

It was not all that
Apparent
To those around him

But it was happening
It was over a period
Of years

Even after it was too late

Even years later

And then it became clear
To some
Not all

Maybe a few months
Before he died
He stole a pocket comb
A man of genius

Turiddu, che cos'hai fattu?

PROMISE

9:47 am, March 17, 2015
St. Patrick's Day

I was just sitting
On my patio
Looking at the trees
The fruit trees

It's Springtime
There's a newness of life

The tender green leaves
On the persimmon tree
Hold a special meaning
Of freshness
Of newness
Of rebirth
Not just birth
But rebirth

And then I saw
Their specialness
And inspiration

As beautiful as birth is
Rebirth is more
It holds promise
As if lifting oneself
From a slumber
And more

WHOOPING COUGH

9:30 am, Palm Sunday
March 29, 2015

It was in the 1920s
My brothers and I
Walking on a street
In Lyndhurst, New Jersey

We were whooping away
We had the whooping cough

It was in the cold of winter
We, each of us,
Wearing heavy overcoats
Walking together
Alone
The four of us

Ages two or three to
Nine or ten

The freedom of those days

Oh, how I would like
To be able to see
Those four overcoats

Chaos exploded in the thirties

All gone

SPECIFIC TRAITS

1:14 pm, Palm Sunday
March 29, 2015

We are in a state
Of befuddlement

One morning
In the early nineteen fifties
I walked into
The outpatient clinic

And was greeted by
The hospital superintendent
A psychiatrist
Who asked me to see
What I could do
With a six year old boy
He had tried to deal with
That is
Do psychotherapy
Of some kind

The child was unresponsive
Sitting in a little chair

Feeling that I had been given
Carte Blanche,
As they say,
I felt pretty confident
I was in my early thirties

So I strode in
Picked the boy up
And proceeded to
Place him on my lap

He went bananas

And so, there it was
My introduction to the world
Of autism

At the time it was quite new
There was thought to be
Only a few in the
Whole country

Today, in the twenty-first
Century
We know
A lot more

We know that
There is some sort of barrier
Between the autistic person
That is, someone
So diagnosed
And other people

But, really

We know that such a person
Is unskilled
In the area of
Human relations

Can be fearful
Hesitant
Ah yes!
Befuddled

Lately, it has been noted
Some such people
Might be geniuses

A curve of distribution
Tells us how many people
There are
Who possess a particular
Trait
And the height
Of that curve
Tells us how many
There are
At different degrees

The normal curve
Or bell curve
Or Gaussian curve
Shows us

Where height is concerned
Or weight
Or whatever

We typically find
That most people
Fall into the average
Range

Where autism is concerned
It seems
That we could
Measure people

Even those not so
Considered

On a range
Of clumsiness
In human relations

We need not call names
Anymore
That is, idiots

In the past
Geniuses like
Anton Bruckner
Were considered, and called,
Idiots

And Thomas Aquinas
A brilliant man
A doctor of the church
A saint, even

We need to look at
Specific traits
Especially clumsiness
In human relations

We need to look at
Specific traits

MUSLIM LEADERS

8:24 am, Good Friday
April 13, 2015

This morning's paper reports
The massacre of 147
Students
At a university in Kenya

They were Christians, very possibly
Catholic

Their fellow students who were
Muslim
Were spared

The killers were Muslim
And meanwhile, I sit here
In comfort
In America

And Muslim leaders
In America
Say
They're peace-loving

I wonder what it would be like
If they were not

GAYETANA TORRES

4:50 pm, Friday
April 17, 2015

Gayetana Torres
Was the mother of
Lucy Mendoza

She died November 16, 1991
Born in Mexico
On August 14, 1899

She was ninety-two

We, of course,
Went to her funeral

We didn't know her much
But she was the mother of
Our friend

And it strikes me
That she lived simply
And quietly
No fuss

Not like those of us
Of a similar age

A quiet
Dignified
Lady

ANDREW

8:50 am, Monday
April 20, 2015

Andrew Aguanno was
A Sicilian
Born in New York City
But raised in Sicily

As his wife, Vita, had been

We had gotten to
Know him
And his family
His brother Filippo
And the rest
In Southern California

Through my brother

They'd all of them come
To our anniversary parties

And, as life would have it,
We came to this point
Where Andrew was in
The hospital in Burbank
Quite serious

And I was asked
By his family
To come

When I arrived I found
A large number of them
In the hospital waiting room
And I was immediately
Ushered into Andrew's room
Where I visited with him,
A gentle soul,
And left

Back in the waiting room
It soon developed
That food had been brought in
And Andrew would not eat of it

Again, I was urged to
Do something

So, back to his room
Where he was sitting
In a wheelchair
And I put my arm
Around him
And said,
"Andrew, you should eat."

And he, gentle and patient
With me
Made some effort
In that direction

Andrew died
The next day, I think
And at the rosary
The next evening
His brother-in-law, Gasper,
Told me and my brother

That Andrew had said to him,
"Gasper,
I'm seventy-five
Don't you think it's time
For me to die?"

The next day was his funeral
At St. Patrick's, I think.
And as the funeral procession
Was moving down the aisle
His wife, Vita,

Who had been born in the
Same apartment house
And raised in Sicily as he was
Now, his widow,
And following his coffin
Cried out,
"Andrew, Andrew, I love
you all my life."

EVER SO BRIEFLY

3:52 pm, Wednesday
April 29, 2015

Some ten or
Twenty years ago
I was driving home
Going West on
The freeway

After a two-hour visit
At the Norton Simon Museum
In Pasadena

I had been there
For two hours
Standing and looking
At the paintings therein

I have always found it
Trying

Anyway,
I was now
Driving westward
Confronted by
These awesome clouds
Unbelievably breathtaking

And I realized
That the beauty of creation
Of such a sight
Could never be matched
By paintings in a museum

That creation
Dwarfs us and
Our creations
So easily

So massively did it
Register itself

And suddenly
I decided to stop by
St. Joseph's hospital
In Burbank to visit
Ann Caiozzo
Who lay dying

The victim of a
Dental procedure
Gone awry

Endocarditis

When I arrived at
Her bedside
Stunned to see that
No one was there

I learned,
Perhaps later,
That while she lay
In a coma

(She had been a member
Of St. Charles' choir
Conducted by the superb
Paul Salamunovich)

That Paul had visited
And when told that
He was visiting her
She came out

Ever so briefly
From her coma

LOST, FORGOTTEN

1:30 pm, Friday
May 9, 2015

It's a part of life
There's not much to be
Done about it

I don't know what
To call it
A sadness
A poignancy

It is, on the surface,
The passage of time

But, there's more to it

Friends is what it is
The separation from friends

Society has become
More mobile
Than you once thought

Those childhood friends
Vanished
When there could have been
Should have been
More to them

But the Army
That's what I've been
Thinking about

Of course, we were young

Jimmy Stampolis
Frank de Maria
Steve Taktekos, Hank Belluscio
Mike Graziano, Al Dennehey
George Terpak, Dan Daiuto

Some of us were
In the war together

You don't forget that

And the many more
Who were buddies
To ones whose names

I've forgotten

That, too

ROOTS

10:22 am, Thursday
May 14, 2015

Roots there were
Valued
Sentimental

Emotional ties
Recognized
Valued

And many there were

But with structure
Unmaintained
Not fully recognized

No, not maintained

In the end
Not strong enough
To hold one in place

And, a sad
Separation
Departure

THE BIRDS ARE SINGING

7:53 am, Tuesday
May 26, 2015

The birds are singing
As they do
Most mornings
Or every morning

The songs of birds
That are free

A gift to me

Freely given

JIMMY STAMPOLIS

9:15 am, Friday
May 29, 2015

I have a 10 o'clock
Appointment
This morning

At the pacemaker clinic
A quarterly thing
To see how it's working
My pacemaker, that is

It's for my heart

And I thought
That I might
Be using
A wheelchair
My wife would be
Pushing it

And then I thought
As I occasionally do
That I might run into
An Army buddy

Old he would be

In this instance
It would be
Jimmy Stampolis

Old now, of course
Like me
Ninety-five

And I would say
To him,
"Jimmy!
Is that you?"

"How are you, Buddy?"

We were in the
Signal Corps together
At Ft. Monmouth
New Jersey

A long time ago

SPANISH

11:05 am, Monday
June 1, 2015

My friend, René,
Was an architect
A former neighbor

And we were good friends
Till his death
A year or two ago

I drove his sons
To choir for a few years
Till René himself
Joined

After moving and
Apparently
Leaving the safety,
The friendly concerns
Of the neighborhood

Having come under the
Influence
Of a builder
Of a fellow Bolivian
Heart surgeon

Matters changed

Lucy, his widow
From Mexico,
Was not the same
Either

And, even
At his funeral

Could speak only
Spanish
To me
A friend of many years

Who is not that great
At Spanish

DECISIONS

11:11 am, Monday
June 1, 2015

Decisions, decisions
People make them

Sort of

I don't know

So many
Poorly

Decisions must be made
Or there is some force there
Impelling

And a lifetime
Is impacted

ALL THE TREES

6:50 am, Saturday
June 20, 2015

This morning
The air is fresh
The birds
All sorts of birds
Are singing

The aroma
Of the gardenias
Is entering
The library
With window
And door open

And all the trees
All the trees

There you have it

LIVELIER BIRDS

6:13 pm, Thursday
July 2, 2015

I was just sitting
On my patio
Six P.M.

And some birds
Were singing
To my surprise

It's hot out
At this time
Probably in the
Low eighties

In the morning
In the cool of
The morning
There are more birds

Much livelier
It's different
Mornings are
Refreshing
Inspiring

BEATIFIC

6:31 pm, Thursday
July 2, 2015

We've had a
Cleaning crew
For five or more years
Once we,
My wife, that is,
Became too old
To cope

They are Salvadorans
Happy to leave
A homeland
Too violent
To abide

And we are friendly
With them

Recently, Alfredo,
One of their number
A gentlemanly
Devout fellow
Was found to have
Cancer

A real blow

And he is receiving
Treatment

And his wife
Martha
Seems to have
Taken his place

And every second week
We, each of us,
Separately
Ask about Alfredo's
Condition

And she gives an
Update

With a smile
That seems to reflect
The presence of God
In all this

Beatific

RESPECT

12:40 pm, Sunday
July 5, 2015

It just came to me
Why would some people
Value money
Or drugs

Or crime
Murder
Stealing

For years
Decades

And many unable
To lift themselves
From the pit
They're in

It's got to do with
Respect

The lack of it

How?
Why?

Father Brennan

MISTAKES

9:48 pm, Thursday
July 9, 2015

It's unbelievable
The mistakes we make

Multitudes of them

As we go through life

You would think they
Are unavoidable

And the dangers
With or without
Mistakes

And yet,
Mistakes are unavoidable
And they play a critical role
In our lives

Yes, a central role
An odd role

It's the acknowledgement
Of mistakes
That's the issue

On the one hand
It's difficult to do
Very difficult

And yet
This admission
Can be the beginning
Of truth

Of wisdom

Honesty and learning

And courage

THE ISSUE

11:00 am, Tuesday
July 21, 2015

This morning
I was reminded
Of an incident
Of years past

I was a recruit
A volunteer
In 1939
And had been placed
In the Medical Corps

And as we,
The soldier medics, one evening,
Were having dinner
We were the late shift
And dinner was a break
Maybe 8 pm

When a fellow
Named Fox
Seated opposite me
I did not know him
Never spoke to him

Suddenly emptied
His coffee cup
At me

There might have been
Twenty or thirty soldiers
There

And they,
While I sat,
Began to shout,
"Fight, fight!"

And we were ushered
On to the large landing
Outside

And I found myself
Standing
And he, Fox,
Rushing murderously
In my direction

And I stood with
My left fist
Sticking out
And he running
Into it

And each time
He did this
I was able to avert
Disaster

And after a few of
These forays
He lay on his back
Covered with blood

And I, not knowing
What to do,
Went over to him
And said,
"Had enough?"
And he hysterically said,
"Yeah, yeah."

And as I walked away
An old soldier
Walked alongside
Saying, "I never saw
          something like that
          ever happen."

And I asked what
He meant
And he said, "Usually
          at a time like this
          the winner stomps
          all over the loser's face."

I went to the hospital
Ward
And asked the young
Nurse lieutenant in charge
For permission to go
To my quarters to change
My coffee-stained uniform
For a fresh one

On my return
I noticed Fox
In an entry office
Giving testimony

And when I reached the ward
This beautiful lieutenant
 Said,
"I'm so proud of you!"

Once in a while
In the seventy-six years
Since
I have wondered why
I did not receive some
Official recognition
Over that incident

Fox was demoted
Stripped of his rank
And, later, when I had to
Deal with what to do
With a soldier who
Had died
He was silently helpful

And this morning
I realized
That I had received
Ample recognition

That old soldier
That pretty lieutenant
Were bearing witness
That they were
Witnessing angels

And I had failed
To see

God doesn't work
Through official
Agencies or channels

He, who believes in freedom,
Was expressing
His own

Currently, there is,
In the media
A tragic story

A woman in her
Twenties, late twenties

A black woman
An African-American
Or such

Has died in jail

And there is some
Dispute
As to the how and why

And, of course,
This is America
The focus is on the
Whys and hows, etc.
Of this tragedy

She appears to have
Committed suicide

But, the investigation continues

The issue underlying
Is, of course,
Racism

That is,
In the media's eyes

But I say the issue
Is freedom

A human being is meant
To be free

God made us for freedom
And to deprive a person
Of freedom
Is contrary to
God's plan

Island

INSCRUTABLE

8:02 am, Thursday
July 30, 2015

This morning
God seems
Inscrutable
To me

It's simple enough
But opaque

Someone whose life
Is a shambles
Shambles all about her

I turn to my wife
"She made her choices,"
She says

That's simple
Free will it is

I don't know

A BEAUTIFUL SMILE

9:35 am, Wednesday
August 26, 2015

A few days ago
At 5 o'clock Mass
I found myself
Sitting in a pew
In front of a fellow
Who I'd once been
In the men's choir with

I don't remember ever
Talking to him

The men's choir
Was disbanded
Years ago

Anyway,
Over the past few years
I'd noticed him
At Mass

He seems to be going
To daily Mass

And he has grown
A beard

Kind of seclusive
In manner

He may be a widower

Anyway, I turned around
At a certain point
And told him
"You were in the choir."

And he acknowledged
That he had been
And then remembered me

And with one of
The most beautiful
Smiles

I could not have
Predicted it

IN FUTURE

11:21 am, Sunday
September 13, 2015

I was driving home
This morning

And having difficulty
As usual

I would rather not be
Driving
At my age
But that is the world
We live in

Machines
Mechanization

A far cry
From years past
When horses were about

And I was wondering,
In future
What it would be like

People being more
Automated
Themselves

CI SUGNU MUNTAGNI

11:39 am, Sunday
September 13, 2015

My father-in-law
Was a quiet man

At least, when I knew him
Meeting him when he was
Fifty-three
And I was courting
His daughter

He had come from Sicily
When he was twelve
Alone

He seemed to be pleased
And peaceful
Often smiling

But not much talking

One day, twelve years or so
After our first meeting
And they were visiting us
In California

I arrived from work
To find that he had
He had cut my lemon tree
To about 10 inches off the ground

He said nothing
I said nothing
Though I'd thought
He'd killed my tree

In truth
He had saved the tree
Which had been on the
Verge of dying

And he
The Sicilian
Knew what he was doing

The tree is alive today

And then there was that time
Perhaps the only time
When something
I don't know what
Perturbed him
And he said gruffly,

"Ci sugnu muntagni"

Legends

DAWN

6:08 am, Thursday
October 1, 2015

It's fascinating
It's fascinating the way
The light comes
Ever so slowly
In the morning

It's dawn
The dawning
Of a new day

So peaceful

By itself
It asks nothing

It says "peace"
That's all

HEROES

8:25 am, Tuesday
October 6, 2015

I was thinking
Just now
Of the time
Two or more years ago

When I was invited
To a place outside
Detroit

Where a holocaust museum
Was being dedicated

They had gotten my name
From some Army orders
Wherein I was
In command of a
Small group of
German Jews

My expenses
And those of my family
Would be paid for

And speaking to
Someone there
In Michigan

I had to decline
I was already, as they say,
Quite advanced in age

Anyway, I was being
Regarded as a hero

There were
Thirteen million Americans
In the service
In the Second World War

They were all heroes

Pretty much

NINETY-FIVE

3:56 pm, Saturday
October 10, 2015

I feel like
A caricature
Of myself

Here I go walking
Pretending to walk

I have to use
A cane

I'm in pain
But cannot
Cry out

It would be
Unseemly

I go about this way
Like others of
My age
Or near to

I'm ninety-five

Liberty Bell

SUPPORT

8:26 am, Saturday
October 24, 2015

Some many years ago
I had a young couple
Come to see me

Their marriage was
In trouble

I saw them only
Briefly
And I have reason
To believe
They later divorced

They had been married
Maybe five years
Arrived in California
Los Angeles
And the marriage
Began to fall apart
Here

They had come from
New York City
My hometown

They were Jewish

Now, New York
When I was growing up
There
Had, as Mayor La Guardia
Used to say,
Eight million people
Who lived in harmony

Two million were Jewish
Two million Irish
Two million Italians
And two million
Of various origins

And each of those groups
Was somewhat tight-knit
And supportive
Bolstering

And this young couple
Had lost theirs

DESTINED?

4:18 pm, Monday
November 16, 2015

I've just begun
Listening
To Bruckner's 7th

A great work
Powerful
Courageous
Ground-breaking

And yet written
By a man
Too timid
To find a wife

Too limited
Too ignorant

And yet
A genius

Was he made
For what he accomplished?

Was this destined?

A WEEK OR SO BEFORE

9:13 am, Wednesday
November 18, 2015

Last night
I was on the phone
With my daughter
My eldest

And,
A propos
Of something

I was telling her
A story of something
I'd experienced
Years past

It was after the Battle
Of St. Lo

The emergence
From Normandy

For perhaps the only time
In the war
Quite a few
Intelligence teams
Came together

The officers were
In a large tent
And the enlisted men
All non-commissioned officers
Were in a large tent
To do their work

The officers were almost all
Lieutenants
A few captains
And one, a major
Who was automatically
In charge
By virtue of his rank
And he wanted things done
A certain way

He wanted all the
Officers
In the smaller tent
Drinking, I believe

I refused
Not openly
If I remember

For a few weeks, perhaps,
He must not have known
What to do

But then he did
He got rid of me

Sent me back to
Military Intelligence
Headquarters

Now, that sounds simple

It wasn't

I reported at
Intelligence headquarters
To a WAC captain
A woman
I was mortified
And, immediately,
That same day
I put in for a transfer
Back to the combat zone
I was young

And, a month or so later,
My request was granted

Too late, I had discovered
That life outside Paris
Was not so bad

And now I arrived
At nineteenth corps
Ninth Army
In Holland

A week or so before
The Battle of the Bulge

Battle of the Bulge

NO

9:17 am, Saturday
November 21, 2015

One day
Many years
Perhaps fifty or
Sixty years ago

When with some
New friends
Bill, a psychologist
Or psychologist intern

And his wife, Dora

I was apparently
Talking or describing
Something ideal
About men

That is my impression

When, suddenly,
Dora blurted out
In a kind of desperation,
"They're not all
That way."

IT WOULDN'T EXIST

4:06 pm, Wednesday
December 2, 2015

I was just now
Sitting in my library
Reading
And listening to music

I had on this CD
I hadn't played
For years

After three or four pieces
I heard the
Intermezzo
From Mascagni's
Cavalleria

And I paid attention
Stopped reading

And it was beautiful

And I thought
If someone hadn't
Set down to write
This music
It wouldn't exist.

TALK

9:42 am, Monday
December 14, 2015

Margaret Chase Smith
A Maine senator
Was quoted as saying
That there is much
Talking
And not enough
Thinking

Oh, how true
This blessed country

Faltering so badly
In its promise

A promise of freedom
Of free speech

Yes
Freedom, freedom

But little true
Freedom

Freedom of speech
So readily surrendered

Freedom of thought
Is a stranger
On these
Our golden shores

There is a ban on thought
That goes unrecognized

But talking continues
Regardless

And people inept
Too beset by problems
That leave little
Room

For vision
For thought
For courage
For integrity

I LOVE THIS WORLD

8:53 am, Saturday
December 19, 2015

I love this world
The aliveness of it

The trees
The flowers
The seasons
The drama
The excitement of it

The homes
The furniture
The plans, designs

The people
Yes, the people
All the drama
The suffering
The brutality
The escaping of refugees
The aloneness
Screams out
Their preciousness

AWARENESS

7:16 am, Tuesday
December 29, 2015

I was just now
Sitting in my library
Looking out the windows
The trees
The skies

And thinking

Of friends in the past

And the smoking
That did them in

And of my experiences
In the Army
In the war
And of a cigarette industry
Generous with their
Cigarettes

One morning I smoked
A whole pack
And then again
A few days later

And that was enough
For me

There was an awareness
Some kind of awareness

And from whence
Did it come?

I think my mother
Taught me
Awareness

And my father, too

Not directly
Oh no

Not directly

Certainly not

TESTIMONY

10:52 am, Saturday
January 9, 2016

I happened
A bit ago
To recall
An experience
Thirty or more years ago

A physician acquaintance
Of mine
Mal

Who urged me
A number of times
To meet with a
Psychiatrist friend of his

Who was in the same
Building
As I was
Two floors above

A nice fellow
Who had a tennis court
In his backyard

And, eventually, I did
We planned to
Have lunch together
At his office
It turned out
Because he was too busy
To go elsewhere

But only for a half hour

And, after talking
I suppose
I began to take my leave

And as I approached
His office door, he said,
"Say, do you do abortions?"

I didn't know what
He was talking about

He explained
That all I would have to do
Was sign a slip of paper

Testifying that the
Pregnant woman was
Too upset
Or something

And for each such
Signature
I would get
Fifty dollars

I never saw him again
Don't remember his name
But, I suppose
He liked to play tennis
And did

And, also, this morning
I had been thinking
That in our present
Culture, so called
We have developed
An accrediting system
Wherein people wear
Shields, or plaques
Or something

Saying they are
Qualified

As physicians, psychologists,
Ministers, priests
Mechanics, etc., etc.

And so they are viewed

But, behind these proclamations
Is a person

And that person has all
The attributes
Of that person

Who is doing whatever
He is doing

TO REMAIN AFLOAT

4:55 pm, Wednesday
January 20, 2016

Let's look at it
This way

Say that life is
Like a ship

And the ship's position
Is like a person's position
In life

His goals
His plans
His movement
Or non-movement

In short
His awareness
Or non-awareness
Of these things

And the ship is
Moving
Or standing still

Does a person know
His goals in life
Etc., etc.

Is his goal (or goals)
Apparent to him or not

With or without
Perceived goals
He will find himself
Buffeted about

He will face obstacles
He will be lured
He will be deceived
Etc., etc.

And he had best
Be aware
If he is to remain
Afloat

A MAN OF MANY FACES

11:09 am, Sunday
January 24, 2016

A man of
Many faces
He leaves behind him
A puzzle

There are some who
Think one way
And there are those
Who see it
Differently

Which makes sense
After all
He was different
To different people

So be it

SURFACE

3:46 pm, Monday
February 1, 2016

There is a situation
Existing
Both currently
And long-standing

It's about the
Younger generation
Or is it really
About the modern day

It's about
The surface

The surface
Seeing the surface
And little else

It's a sort of life
The Silicon Valley
And that kind of stuff

When a new
Product
Is introduced
And millions rush
To acquire it

And these people
Know about these products
Or quickly learn

I hope it's not really
As widespread
As one would think
From all the hullabaloo

The issue is really
That such things
Have no true value
No true importance

Except in a largely
Negative way

They are in a surface
Reality

And people develop
A surface kind
Of life
Of wisdom

Actually
We have seen this
Sort of focus
For generations

A rapid knowledge
An immediate response thing

Quick
Not deep

Ignorance of the
Underlying

In relationships even

Chaos

PEOPLE AND THINGS

8:54 am, Saturday
February 6, 2016

I was just now
Looking out
And thinking of
Past experiences
And seeing the trees

And I thought of
People and things
The trees yes
And then
People

The people I've known
The people in my life
And how things have
Turned out

And I saw a distinction
It has to do with
Smallness

Yes, smallness
Of perspective

And then there's instinct

NEVER REALIZED SUCH

9:53 am, Saturday
February 13, 2016

My barber is
From Egypt
Been here for thirty or more
Years
Never been back
He's a Christian

Not long ago
I was sitting
In his barber shop
Awaiting my turn

Near a man
Probably a Mexican
Probably in his
Thirties

I have lately been
Starting conversations
I don't think much
Of sitting in silence
In waiting rooms
And such
And people seem to like it

I must have asked him
A question
Like
Where he was from
Or something
I don't remember

And he said
Prison
And I showed
At least some shock

And I asked why
And he said
Manslaughter
And I expressed
Somehow
Amazement
And asked how

And he told me
That a man in a setting
Perhaps one like we were in
That day

Had shown some disrespect
For his wife
Sitting with him
And their daughter
And started to walk
Quickly away

And he, the man I was
Talking with,
Being some kind of guard
And carrying a gun
Pursued and shot him

And I expressed amazement
And indicated that he
Had been stupid
Which he admitted

In the ensuing discussion
He expressed some
Negative impression
Of the police

And I told him how
Different were
Our most recent wars
In which our soldiers could be
In a supposedly
Peaceful, friendly situation,
Only to be attacked, killed
By people in disguise
And that this hadn't been
True
For those of us in
The second World War
And that our police
Were in situations
Similar to our most recent
Experiences
And he thanked me
And he said he had never
Realized such

PREVIOUS BOOKS BY THE AUTHOR

Unlike the Vikings

Casta Diva

GrandMa and the Miracles

The Bird and the Squirrel

Rosalie Was All Night Without the Light

Chocolate and Cigarettes

The Snow Was Falling

RIVERSHORE BOOKS

Website:
www.rivershorebooks.com

Blog:
blog.rivershorebooks.com

Facebook:
www.facebook.com/rivershore.books

Twitter:
www.twitter.com/rivershorebooks

Email:
Jansina@rivershorebooks.com

www.ingramcontent.com/pod-product-compliance
Lightning Source LLC
Chambersburg PA
CBHW071612040426
42452CB00008B/1324